DATE DUE

Bilingual Edition

READING POWER

Edición Bilingüe

Dale Earnhardt, Jr.

NASCAR Road Racer
Piloto de NASCAR

Rob Kirkpatrick

Traducción al español
Mauricio Velázquez de León

The Rosen Publishing Group's
PowerKids Press™ & **Buenas Letras**™
New York

1

921
EAR
C.1
11.95
2003

For my grandmother, Irene.
Para mi Abuela Irene.

Published in 2002 by The Rosen Publishing Group, Inc.
29 East 21st Street, New York, NY 10010

First Bilingual Edition 2002
First Edition in English 2001
Revised Edition 2002

Book design: Maria Melendez

Photo Credits: pp. 5, 22 © Jamie Squire/Allsport; pp. 7, 9, 11, 21 © David
Taylor/Allsport; p. 13 © Craig Jones; pp. 15, 17 © Jon Ferrey/Allsport; p. 19 ©
Matthew Stockman/Allsport.

Text Consultant: Linda J. Kirkpatrick, Reading Specialist/Reading Recovery Teacher

Kirkpatrick, Rob.
    Dale Earnhardt, Jr. : NASCAR road racer = Dale Earnhardt, Jr. : piloto de
NASCAR / Rob Kirkpatrick : traducción al español Mauricio Velázquez de León.
    p. cm. — (Reading power)
    Includes index.
    SUMMARY: A simple introduction to the NASCAR driver who is the son of another
winning racer, Dale Earnhardt, Sr.
    ISBN 0-8239-6146-X (lib. bdg.)
    1. Earnhardt, Dale, Jr. Juvenile literature. 2. Automobile racing drivers—United
States Biography Juvenile literature. [1. Earnhardt, Dale, Jr. 2. Automobile racing
drivers. 3. Spanish language materials—Bilingual.] I. Title. II. Series.
    GV1032.E18 K57 1999
    796.72'092—dc21
    [B]

Word Count:
English: 132
Spanish: 146

Manufactured in the United States of America

Contents

Contenido

Dale Earnhardt, Jr. races cars.

———————

Dale Earnhardt, Jr. es corredor de autos.

4

The cars in races have numbers on them. Dale had a car with number 31.

Los autos de carreras tienen números. Dale tenía el número 31 en su automóvil.

Dale has number 3 on his car now. He drives a Chevrolet.

Ahora su auto lleva el número 3. Maneja un Chevrolet.

Some cars can get very close in a race. Dale likes his car to be in front.

A veces los autos se acercan mucho durante las carreras.
A Dale le gusta que su auto vaya al frente.

Lots of people like to see
Dale race. They like to see
him drive fast.

———————

A mucha gente le gusta
ver manejar a Dale.
Los aficionados disfrutan
cuando maneja rápido.

People help Dale in races.
He makes a pit stop when
he needs help with his car.

Hay personas que
ayudan a Dale en las
competiciones. Hace una
parada en los *pits*
cuando necesita ayuda
con su auto.

Sometimes, Dale needs
new tires. New tires can
help Dale drive fast.

————————

A veces el auto de Dale
necesita cambiar llantas.
Las llantas nuevas
lo ayudan a
manejar más rápido.

In 1998, Dale won a big race. The race was the Diehard 250.

En 1998, Dale ganó una carrera muy importante. Esa carrera se llama *Diehard 250.*

Dale needs to have a helmet, goggles, and a mike for his races.

———————

Dale necesita un casco, unos anteojos protectores y un micrófono para sus carreras.

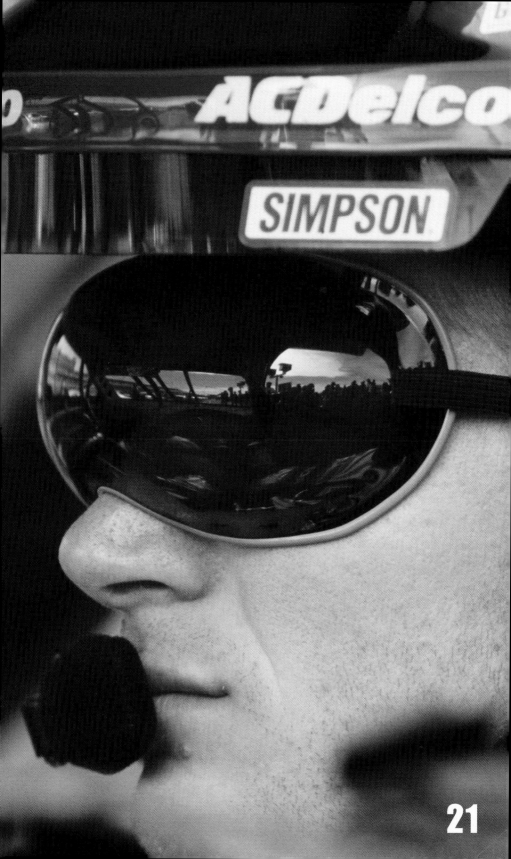

Dale's father was a race car driver, too. His name was Dale also.

El papá de Dale también fue corredor de autos. Su nombre también era Dale.

Here are more books to read about the Earnhardts:

Para leer más acerca de los Earnhardts, te recomendamos estos libros:

Dale Earnhardt, Jr. (NASCAR Track Sounds). Futech Interactive Products

Dale Earnhardt, Sr. (NASCAR Track Sounds). Futech Interactive Products

To learn more about NASCAR, check out this Web site:

Para aprender más sobre NASCAR, visita esta página de Internet:

http://sikids.com/racing/overdrive/index.html

Glossary

Chevrolet (shev-roh-LAY) The name of a type of car.

goggles (GAH-gulz) What a driver wears to keep his eyes safe.

helmet (HEL-mit) What a driver wears to keep his head safe.

mike (MYK) What a driver uses so he can talk to his crew while driving.

pit stop (PIT STOP) When a driver goes off the track to get car fixed.

Index

Glosario

anteojos protectores (los) Tipo de lentes que usa un corredor de autos para proteger los ojos.

casco (el) Lo que usa un corredor de autos para proteger la cabeza.

Chevrolet Una marca de auto.

micrófono (el) Lo que usa un corredor de autos para poder hablar con su equipo mientras maneja.

parada de pits Cuando un piloto sale de la pista para arreglar o abastecer su auto.

Índice